AI Tax Strategy, Entity Selection & Profit Shielding

How Smart Structuring Cuts Your Tax Bill

AF849259

By Joe Co

Published by Live Stronger Faster

Copyright © 2026 by Joe Correa

All rights reserved.

No part of this publication may be reproduced, distributed, or transmitted in any form or by any means—electronic, mechanical, photocopying, recording, or otherwise—without the prior written permission of the publisher, except in the case of brief quotations embodied in critical reviews and certain other noncommercial uses permitted by copyright law.

This book is for educational and informational purposes only. The author and publisher are not engaged in rendering legal, financial, tax, or other professional advice. Readers should consult a qualified professional before making any financial decisions.

First Edition

Table of Contents

Introduction

In the modern business world, taxes are no longer jus something you calculate at the end of the year — they ar something you engineer in advance. Every choice a busines makes, from how it is structured to how it pays its owners, t how it reports income and expenses, directly determines hov much profit it gets to keep. Yet most business owners stil operate as if taxes are fixed and unavoidable, believing tha high revenue automatically means high taxes. This book i written to permanently eliminate that belief. Artificia intelligence has now transformed tax strategy into a precisio science where legal structures, cash flow, payroll, an distributions can be continuously optimized in real time Instead of reacting to taxes after they happen, AI allow business owners to design their tax outcome before the incom even arrives. Book 7 exists to show how entity selection ownership design, and profit-shielding strategies powered b artificial intelligence can reduce taxes dramatically whil staying fully compliant with the law, turning taxes from a cos into a controllable variable in the business equation.

For decades, tax planning was something only th ultra-wealthy could afford. Large corporations hired teams o attorneys and accountants to design complex structures tha minimized taxes while protecting assets. Small business owners and entrepreneurs, by contrast, were left with generic advice like "form an LLC" or "talk to a CPA," without any way to see how different structures would actually impact their real numbers. Artificial intelligence has now closed that gap. Today, AI models can simulate thousands of entity combinations, ownership structures, compensation strategies, and profit-distribution scenarios in seconds. They can instantly compare how a sole proprietorship, LLC, S-corporation, C-corporation, partnership, or holding company structure would perform under different income levels, different states, and different business models. This means that even a one-person online business can now design tax strategies that rival those of multinational corporations. This book shows you how to use AI not only to choose the right entity, but to continuously evolve your structure as your business grows so that taxes never erode your success.

Most business owners unknowingly choose the worst possible tax structure. They form the wrong type of entity, pay themselves the wrong way, and mix personal and business finances in ways that create unnecessary tax exposure. Some end up paying self-employment tax on income that could have been shielded. Others miss payroll strategies that could save tens of thousands of dollars per year. Still others operate profitable companies but never create the asset-protection layers that separate personal wealth from business risk. AI changes all of this by making structural planning visual, dynamic, and data-driven. Instead of guessing or relying on outdated rules of thumb, business owners can now see exactly how every dollar flows through their entity structure, how much is taxed, how much is shielded, and how much ends up in their pocket. This book teaches you how to build those flows so that profits are maximized and taxes are minimized by design.

Entity selection is the foundation of tax optimization. Whether you operate as a sole proprietor, LLC, S-corp, C-corp, partnership, or holding company determines how income is taxed, how losses are deducted, and how profits can be distributed. But the best entity for one business may be disastrous for another. A freelancer, an online course creator, a real estate investor, and a SaaS founder all face radically different tax dynamics. AI now makes it possible to evaluate these differences with mathematical precision. It can forecast income, expenses, growth, and distributions and show how each entity type performs over time. This allows entrepreneurs to stop using generic structures and instead build entities that are custom-engineered for their exact business model. In this book, you will learn how AI evaluates these structures, how it identifies hidden tax inefficiencies, and how it recommends optimized legal frameworks that grow more powerful as revenue increases.

Profit shielding is where tax strategy becomes wealth strategy. Profit shielding refers to the legal techniques that keep business income from being exposed to unnecessary taxation while simultaneously protecting it from lawsuits, creditors, and financial risk. This includes strategies such as reasonable salary optimization, profit distributions, management companies, intellectual property holding entities, retirement structures, and reinvestment vehicles. Traditionally, these strategies were difficult to coordinate and easy to misapply. Artificial intelligence now integrates all of them into a unified financial model that shows how profits move from one entity to another, how taxes are triggered or avoided, and how capital is preserved. This means you can now design systems where income flows through protective channels, minimizing both tax and risk. This book will show you how to build these structures step by step using AI-driven modeling, ensuring every dollar of profit is working for you instead of against you.

One of the most powerful advantages of AI-based tax strategy is timing. Taxes are deeply affected by when income is received, when expenses are deducted, and when profits are distributed. Traditional accounting looks backward, telling you what already happened. AI looks forward, allowing you to shift income, accelerate deductions, delay taxes, and strategically time transactions so that the tax burden is minimized. For example, AI can determine whether it is better to pay yourself a bonus this year or next year, whether to expense or depreciate an asset, or whether to reinvest profits through a specific entity. These decisions, when optimized correctly, can save more money than most businesses ever realize. This book teaches you how to use AI forecasting to control tax timing with surgical precision, ensuring that your cash flow is always aligned with your long-term financial strategy.

AI also introduces continuous optimization into tax planning. Most businesses only review their tax strategy once a year, often after it is too late to change anything. With AI, tax strategy becomes a living system that updates as income, expenses, payroll, and growth patterns change. If revenue spikes, AI adjusts compensation strategies. If expenses increase, it reallocates deductions. If you expand into a new state or country, it recalculates entity efficiency. This creates a self-correcting financial architecture that constantly adapts to keep taxes as low as legally possible. In this book, you will learn how to set up these AI-driven monitoring systems so that your entity structure and profit-shielding strategy remain optimized at all times, without manual recalculations or guesswork.

Ultimately, Book 7 is about transforming your business into a financial fortress. Revenue alone does not create wealth — what matters is how much you keep and how well it is protected. Artificial intelligence now gives business owners the same strategic advantage that once belonged only to elite financial institutions. By combining entity selection, profit-shielding structures, and AI-driven forecasting, you can build a business that grows faster, pays less in taxes, and retains more capital for reinvestment and personal wealth. This book is your blueprint for that transformation. As you move forward, you will learn not only how to choose the right entity, but how to turn your entire business into a machine that legally minimizes taxes, maximizes profits, and shields everything you have worked so hard to build.

Chapter 1

The Hidden Tax Engine Inside Every Business

Every business, whether it earns ten thousand dollars a year or ten million, runs on an invisible engine that determines how much money it truly makes. This engine is not marketing, sales, or operations — it is tax structure. Two companies can generate the same revenue, have the same expenses, and even serve the same customers, yet one can keep twice as much profit simply because its legal and tax architecture was built correctly. Most entrepreneurs never see this engine. They operate their business on the surface level, focused on income and growth, while the tax system quietly drains money beneath them. Artificial intelligence has now made this hidden engine visible. It allows business owners to see exactly how their structure converts revenue into after-tax wealth, revealing inefficiencies that once went unnoticed for years.

The traditional way of choosing a business entity has always been dangerously oversimplified. People are told to form an LLC for protection, an S-corporation for tax savings, or a C-corporation for growth, without any real analysis of how these structures interact with their specific income, payroll, state taxes, or future plans. AI eliminates this guesswork. It can simulate how every dollar moves through each type of entity, how much tax is triggered at each stage, and how different compensation methods change the final outcome. Instead of vague advice, business owners now receive precise financial blueprints. They can see in advance how their choices will affect their tax bill five years into the future, not just this quarter.

At the core of every entity structure are three powerful forces: taxation, liability, and flexibility. Taxation determines how income is taxed. Liability determines what happens if the business is sued or fails. Flexibility determines how easily money can move between the business and the owner. Most entrepreneurs unknowingly sacrifice at least one of these. A sole proprietor may enjoy simplicity but pays high self-employment tax. A C-corporation may offer growth benefits but exposes owners to double taxation. An improperly structured LLC may offer liability protection but miss massive tax savings. AI analyzes all three forces at once and shows how to balance them for maximum advantage.

One of the most overlooked tax leaks in small and mid-sized businesses is owner compensation. How you pay yourself is just as important as how much you earn. Salary, distributions, bonuses, reimbursements, and retirement contributions all have different tax consequences. AI can evaluate every option and calculate the most efficient mix. It can determine the legally lowest taxable income while still allowing you to access cash when you need it. This means that instead of blindly paying yourself a salary or taking random draws, you operate with a tax-optimized compensation strategy that adapts as your income grows.

Profit shielding is the next layer of this hidden engine. Shielding does not mean hiding money or breaking the law — it means placing profits inside structures that reduce exposure to taxation and risk. This includes management companies, intellectual property entities, retirement vehicles, and reinvestment accounts. AI models can show how profits should flow between these entities to minimize taxes while maximizing asset protection. Instead of piling income into one vulnerable business, money moves through a system designed to preserve it.

What makes AI revolutionary is that it removes emotion from financial decisions. Business owners often resist restructuring because they fear complexity or think their business is "too small." AI doesn't care about fear — it only sees numbers. It shows that even a $100,000-a-year business can save thousands with the right entity strategy, while a $1 million business can save hundreds of thousands. This creates clarity, allowing entrepreneurs to make confident, data-driven decisions.

Another powerful benefit of AI is scenario testing. What happens if your revenue doubles? What if you move to another state? What if you sell part of your company? What if you bring in investors? AI can model all of these events and show how your tax structure responds. This allows you to design a structure that is not just good today, but resilient in the future.

When you combine entity optimization, compensation design, and profit shielding into one AI-driven system, taxes stop being an afterthought and become a strategic weapon. You no longer wonder how much you will owe — you know. You no longer fear tax season — you control it. This is the hidden engine of wealth, and once it is activated, every dollar you earn works harder for you.

"The Two Businesses on the Same Street"

Michael and David owned nearly identical digital marketing agencies on the same street in Austin, Texas. Both served local businesses, both charged similar fees, and both earned just over $500,000 a year in revenue. On paper, they looked like equals. But when tax season arrived, Michael felt a knot in his stomach while David calmly smiled. Michael owed nearly $140,000 in taxes. David owed less than half that. Michael couldn't understand how it was possible. Michael had formed a simple LLC years earlier because someone online told him it was the safest option. He paid himself whenever he needed money and assumed that taxes were just the cost of success. David, however, had used AI-powered tax modeling to design his business from the inside out. He operated an S-corporation for his agency, paid himself a strategic salary, and routed profits through a holding company that reduced his tax exposure. Every decision was backed by numbers.

One afternoon, Michael finally asked David how he was keeping so much more of his money. David opened his laptop and showed him a dashboard. It displayed income, payroll, distributions, taxes, and projected savings five years into the future. David explained that AI was constantly recalculating his structure based on real-time financial data. When revenue increased, the system adjusted how he paid himself. When expenses changed, deductions were optimized. His business was running on autopilot.

Michael realized that he had been operating blind. His business made money, but it leaked profits through inefficient tax design. With David's help, he ran his own numbers through the same AI model. The results shocked him. By restructuring his LLC into an S-corp and optimizing his compensation, he could save over $60,000 per year. By adding a profit-shielding entity, he could protect his earnings from lawsuits and future tax increases. Six months later, Michael felt like he was running a completely different company. His revenue was the same, but his bank account was larger. His stress was gone. And for the first time, he understood that real business success wasn't just about making money — it was about keeping it. The two businesses on the same street were no longer equal. One was still paying blindly. The other was building wealth with intelligence.

Chapter 2

Choosing the Right Entity: How AI Designs Your Tax Identity

Every business is born into the tax system the moment it earn its first dollar, but how that dollar is treated depends entirel on the legal identity the business wears. That identity – whether a sole proprietorship, LLC, S-corporation C-corporation, partnership, or holding company — acts like a lens through which the tax code sees your company. Th wrong lens distorts profits into taxable income, while the righ one bends cash flow into legally protected wealth. For decades entrepreneurs were forced to guess which entity was best fo them, relying on generic advice or outdated rules of thumb Artificial intelligence now replaces that guesswork wit precision. It evaluates income, growth rates, payroll needs investor plans, and state taxes to create a tailored tax identit that matches the reality of your business.

A sole proprietor is the simplest form of business, bu simplicity is expensive. Every dollar earned is subject to income tax and self-employment tax, which means hig earners can lose more than thirty percent of their profit before they ever reach a personal bank account. An LLC provides legal protection, but unless it is taxed strategically, i often changes nothing about how much tax is paid. An S-corporation allows owners to split income between salary and distributions, reducing self-employment tax. A C-corporation allows profits to be reinvested at lower corporate tax rates. Partnerships allow income to flow in flexible ways. AI compares all of these structures side by side using real numbers rather than assumptions. It shows exactly how much tax each structure produces at different income levels, allowing business owners to see which entity truly serves them best.

What makes AI so powerful in entity selection is that it models the future, not just the present. A business that earns $100,000 today may earn $1 million in three years. A freelancer may become a SaaS founder. A local shop may expand across state lines. Each of these changes alters the optimal tax structure. AI projects revenue growth, expense patterns, and payroll needs and then stress-tests each entity type across those scenarios. This means your business is not just structured for what it is now, but for what it is becoming. The right entity becomes a growth engine rather than a constraint.

Another critical factor is owner compensation. Some entities allow profits to be distributed with little tax. Others require salaries. Some trigger payroll taxes. Some allow income to be deferred. AI evaluates how money flows from the business to the owner under each structure and identifies which method produces the highest after-tax income. This is where massive savings are often found. Two businesses earning the same revenue can see radically different personal income simply because one uses a better-optimized entity.

AI also accounts for state and local taxes, which can dramatically change the outcome. An S-corporation in Florida behaves very differently from one in California. A C-corporation in Texas faces different rules than one in New York. AI integrates these jurisdictional variables into every calculation, ensuring that your structure is not just theoretically good, but locally optimized. This makes it possible to design tax-efficient businesses anywhere in the world.

Holding companies and layered entities take optimization to another level. AI can determine when it makes sense to separate operating income from intellectual property, management fees, or investment income. These structures allow profits to move into lower-tax or more protected entities, shielding them from risk and excessive taxation. Without AI, these systems are complex and error-prone. With AI, they become clean, efficient, and transparent.

The ultimate goal of entity selection is not to avoid taxes, but to align the business with the tax code in a way that rewards growth. The tax system is filled with incentives for certain behaviors — reinvestment, hiring, innovation, and long-term ownership. AI identifies which entities unlock the most incentives for your specific business and builds around them. This turns compliance into a competitive advantage.

By the time a business is fully optimized, its entity structure becomes invisible to outsiders but powerful on the inside. Revenue flows smoothly. Taxes are minimized. Assets are protected. And the business owner gains clarity and confidence, knowing that every dollar earned is being treated in the smartest possible way.

"The Wrong Box"

Elena ran a thriving online coaching business. She had built a loyal following, generated over $700,000 in annual revenue, and worked from home. Yet every year, she felt punished by taxes. Nearly half of what she made disappeared into federal and state obligations. She assumed this was simply the price of success, until a friend suggested she run her numbers through an AI tax modeling system.

The software asked her simple questions: income, expenses, location, future growth plans. Within seconds, it produced a report showing that Elena was trapped in the wrong tax box. She was operating as a single-member LLC taxed like a sole proprietor, paying massive self-employment taxes that could have been avoided. The AI showed her that converting to an S-corporation would allow her to split income into salary and distributions, saving over $50,000 per year. It also revealed that a second holding entity could protect her intellectual property and reduce risk.

Elena was skeptical, but she followed the model. She restructured, adjusted her pay, and separated her brand into a protected entity. When the next tax season arrived, she couldn't believe the difference. Her tax bill was lower, her savings were higher, and her business felt safer.

For the first time, Elena realized that she hadn't been bad at business — she had just been in the wrong box. With AI, she had finally found the one that fit.

Chapter 3

How AI Engineers Your Pay to Minimize Taxes

Most business owners believe that making more money automatically means paying more in taxes, but this is only true when income is paid in the wrong way. The form income takes — salary, distribution, bonus, dividend, reimbursement, or reinvestment — matters just as much as the amount. The tax code treats each form differently, and those differences can be exploited legally and intelligently through artificial intelligence. AI transforms compensation from a guessing game into a precision tool, calculating how every possible way of paying yourself affects both your personal taxes and your business taxes. Instead of reacting to tax bills, business owners can now design how they get paid in a way that keeps more cash in their hands without breaking a single rule.

The most common mistake entrepreneurs make is paying themselves randomly. Some take everything as salary, triggering maximum payroll and self-employment taxes. Others take only distributions, risking penalties and audits. AI eliminates this risk by modeling what the IRS considers reasonable compensation based on industry data, revenue, location, and job role. It then calculates the exact salary level that satisfies compliance while minimizing tax exposure. Thi creates a sweet spot where owners stay protected while legall reducing their tax burden.

Beyond salary and distributions, AI optimizes fringe benefit and reimbursements. Health insurance, retirement plans home office reimbursements, vehicle expenses, and educatio costs can often be paid by the business rather than th individual, creating tax-free or tax-deductible income. A tracks these benefits in real time, ensuring that they ar applied correctly and not overused. This allows busines owners to convert personal expenses into business deductions reducing taxable income without reducing lifestyle.

AI also coordinates compensation with cash flow. Man businesses struggle because owners take too much money ou at the wrong time, starving the business of capital and creatin tax problems. AI forecasting models ensure that payroll distributions, and reinvestment are balanced. It shows when t pay more, when to retain profits, and when to shift incom into future periods. This stabilizes both taxes and operations.

For growing businesses, AI enables compensation layering Owners can be paid through multiple entities — operatin companies, management companies, and holding companie — each with its own tax treatment. AI ensures that these payments are structured correctly, priced at arm's length, and documented properly. This not only reduces taxes but also builds asset protection and audit resistance.

One of the most powerful features of AI is its ability to adapt. If revenue increases, AI adjusts compensation. If expenses rise, it reallocates deductions. If tax laws change, it recalculates the optimal mix. This creates a living compensation system that stays optimized without manual intervention.

Over time, this intelligent pay structure can save tens or even hundreds of thousands of dollars. The business owner is no longer punished for success. Instead, success is rewarded with smarter tax outcomes.

Ultimately, AI turns compensation into a financial control panel. You no longer ask, "How much should I pay myself?" You see the exact answer in real time, backed by data, compliance, and long-term strategy.

"Paid the Wrong Way"

Jason ran a profitable e-commerce brand that sold fitness equipment online. His revenue crossed $1.2 million, yet he felt broke. Every year, his accountant told him he owed more taxes, and Jason simply paid them, assuming it was normal. One day, a friend showed him an AI compensation optimizer.

Jason entered his numbers and watched as the system analyzed his income. The result stunned him. He had been paying himself entirely through salary, triggering massive payroll taxes. The AI recommended a reasonable salary and the rest as distributions, saving him over $80,000 per year. It also showed how his health insurance, vehicle, and home office could be paid by the company.

After implementing the changes, Jason's next tax bill dropped dramatically. His business had not changed — only how he paid himself had. For the first time, he felt in control of his money instead of enslaved by it.

Chapter 4

Profit Shielding: How AI Protects Income Before It Becomes Taxable

Profit shielding is the difference between businesses that grow rich and businesses that merely survive. It is not about hiding income or exploiting loopholes; it is about designing legal pathways where money is earned, moved, and stored in ways that reduce exposure to unnecessary taxation and risk. Most entrepreneurs focus exclusively on revenue generation, believing that taxes are unavoidable consequences of success. In reality, the tax code rewards businesses that structure income intelligently, separate functions strategically, and reinvest profits through approved channels. Artificial intelligence has elevated profit shielding from a complex professional-only discipline into a transparent, measurable, and continuously optimized system available to any business owner willing to model their finances properly.

At its core, profit shielding begins with separation. When income, operations, ownership, and assets are all held inside one entity, that entity becomes both a tax magnet and a liability target. AI immediately identifies this vulnerability by analyzing income concentration, exposure ratios, and tax inefficiencies. It recommends structural separation where appropriate, such as isolating operating revenue from intellectual property, management services, or investment capital. These separations allow income to be recharacterized legally, taxed differently, and protected from lawsuits or business failures. AI does not guess where to split entities; it calculates exactly where the separation produces the greatest reduction in tax exposure while remaining compliant.

One of the most powerful shielding mechanisms is the management company structure. Many businesses unknowingly perform management functions internally that could be compensated separately. AI identifies these functions — administration, branding, licensing, operations, or consulting — and determines whether they can be billed to the operating company at market rates. This shifts profit from high-tax operational income into a management entity that may be taxed more favorably or used for reinvestment. Without AI, these structures are often mispriced or undocumented. With AI, every transaction is modeled, priced, and recorded correctly, dramatically reducing audit risk while increasing tax efficiency.

Intellectual property is another major profit-shielding opportunity that most small and mid-sized businesses ignore. Brands, content, software, training materials, and proprietary systems all represent intellectual property that can be owned separately from the operating business. AI evaluates whether licensing this IP back to the operating entity makes sense financially. When structured properly, licensing fees become deductible expenses for the operating business and income for the IP-holding entity, often taxed at a lower effective rate. AI continuously monitors this arrangement to ensure compliance with valuation standards and regulatory requirements.

Profit shielding also includes reinvestment optimization. The tax code strongly incentivizes businesses to reinvest profits into growth, innovation, and long-term assets. AI identifies which reinvestments produce the highest tax benefit relative to cash outflow. This may include equipment purchases, research and development, technology upgrades, employee benefits, or retirement contributions. By timing and structuring reinvestments correctly, AI ensures that profits are shielded through productive use rather than lost to taxation.

Retirement structures represent one of the most underutilized profit-shielding tools available to business owners. AI models various retirement plans — including solo plans, defined benefit structures, and employer-sponsored options — and determines how much income can be deferred tax-free while aligning with cash flow needs. These structures not only reduce current taxes but also create protected pools of capital that compound over time. AI adjusts contributions dynamically based on income fluctuations, preventing overfunding or missed opportunities.

Another critical layer of profit shielding is timing. Income received today may be taxed differently than income deferred. Expenses deducted now may be more valuable than those taken later. AI models cash flow timing with extraordinary precision, allowing businesses to shift income recognition and expense acceleration legally. This level of control can dramatically smooth tax burdens across years, preventing spikes that strain cash reserves.

What makes AI-driven profit shielding truly transformative is its ability to integrate all these elements into a single system. Instead of isolated strategies managed manually, AI coordinates entity separation, compensation, reinvestment, and timing continuously. If revenue increases, shielding adjusts. If laws change, structures are re-modeled. If risk exposure grows, assets are reallocated. This creates a living financial architecture that protects profits automatically rather than reactively.

Over time, businesses that implement AI-based profit shielding experience compounding advantages. Their tax burden shrinks relative to revenue. Their assets become more secure. Their cash flow becomes predictable. And their owners gain confidence knowing that growth no longer means vulnerability. Profit shielding is not a one-time decision; it is an ongoing strategy, and artificial intelligence is the engine that makes it sustainable, scalable, and safe.

"The Business That Learned How to Keep Its Money"

When Robert started his logistics consulting firm, he believed the only goal was to make as much revenue as possible. And he succeeded. Within five years, his company was earning over two million dollars annually. On the surface, Robert looked successful, but privately he felt trapped. Every year, taxes swallowed a massive portion of his earnings. Lawsuits from dissatisfied clients loomed constantly. His accountant told him everything was normal, that high taxes were simply the price of growth. Robert accepted this explanation until the day his AI financial dashboard showed him the truth.

The system flagged his business with a single warning: "Profit Concentration Risk — Severe." Every dollar Robert earned flowed into one operating entity. That entity owned the contracts, the brand, the systems, and the cash. It paid maximum taxes and carried maximum liability. The AI showed Robert a simulation of a lawsuit wiping out not just his business income, but his personal savings as well. The realization unsettled him deeply. He had built success on a fragile foundation.

The AI proposed a new structure. Robert would keep the operating company lean. A separate management company would handle consulting frameworks, training materials, and operational oversight. His intellectual property — the systems he had developed over years — would be owned by a holding entity and licensed back to the operating business. Each transaction was priced using market data. Each flow was documented. Each entity served a distinct purpose.

At first, Robert feared the complexity. But the AI handled the complexity for him. It generated contracts, tracked payments, monitored compliance, and recalculated tax outcomes continuously. When the structure went live, Robert felt nothing change operationally — except his numbers. His operating company's taxable income dropped significantly. Profits accumulated safely in the holding entity. His personal exposure decreased overnight.

As months passed, the system refined itself. When revenue increased, more profits were routed through licensing. When expenses rose, deductions were optimized. When tax laws shifted, the AI recalculated distributions. Robert stopped worrying about audits because every transaction was justified, documented, and defensible.

The real transformation came during tax season. For the first time, Robert did not feel dread. His tax bill was dramatically lower, but more importantly, his retained earnings were higher than ever. He realized that his business had not learned how to make money — it had learned how to keep it.

Years later, Robert looked back and understood the difference between his old business and his new one. The old business earned income and lost it to taxes and risk. The new business was a system — one that captured value, protected it, and allowed it to grow. Success was no longer fragile. It was engineered.

Chapter 5

Timing, Forecasting, and the AI Advantage in Tax Control

Taxes are not determined solely by how much money a business earns, but by *when* that money is earned, *when* it is recognized, and *when* deductions are applied. Timing is the most underappreciated weapon in tax strategy, yet it is one of the most powerful. Traditional accounting looks backward, reporting what already happened. Artificial intelligence looks forward, allowing businesses to shape outcomes before transactions occur. This shift from historical reporting to predictive control fundamentally changes the tax game. Instead of reacting to tax bills, AI enables business owners to smooth income, accelerate deductions, defer taxable events, and strategically control the rhythm of cash flow so that taxes are minimized legally and sustainably.

At the heart of timing optimization is forecasting. AI analyzes historical income patterns, expense cycles, seasonal revenue swings, payroll obligations, and growth trends to create predictive models that show how future tax liabilities will unfold. These models are not static projections; they adjust continuously as new data arrives. This means business owners can see the tax impact of decisions *before* they make them.

Whether it is signing a new contract, purchasing equipment, hiring staff, or issuing bonuses, AI can show how timing those decisions differently could change the tax outcome dramatically.

Income recognition is one of the most critical timing levers. Depending on the accounting method used, income may be recognized when earned, when invoiced, or when collected. AI evaluates which method aligns best with cash flow and tax minimization goals. In some cases, deferring income into a future period can reduce tax rates or align income with higher deductions. In others, accelerating income may unlock credits or deductions that would otherwise be lost. AI models these scenarios instantly, allowing businesses to choose the most advantageous timing without guesswork.

Expense timing is equally powerful. The tax code allows many expenses to be deducted immediately, while others must be depreciated over time. AI evaluates whether accelerating or spreading deductions produces the best outcome based on projected income. For example, purchasing equipment at the end of a high-income year may generate immediate tax relief, while delaying that purchase may reduce its impact. AI does not rely on rules of thumb; it calculates the precise benefit of each option in the context of the entire financial system. Payroll timing is another critical dimension. Bonuses, raises, and benefit contributions can be timed to shift taxable incom across periods. AI models payroll strategies that balanc employee incentives with tax efficiency, ensuring tha compensation decisions support both morale and financia optimization. This level of coordination is nearly impossibl manually but becomes seamless with AI-driven forecasting.

AI also excels at managing multi-year tax smoothing. Instea of experiencing volatile tax bills that spike unpredictably businesses can use AI to distribute taxable income more evenl over time. This creates stability, improves cash flow planning and reduces financial stress. Predictable taxes allow for bette reinvestment, stronger reserves, and long-term strategi confidence.

What makes AI uniquely powerful is its ability to adapt t change. Tax laws evolve, revenue fluctuates, and busines strategies shift. AI continuously recalibrates forecasts an recommendations in response to these changes. If a nev deduction becomes available, AI incorporates it immediately If a tax rate changes, projections update instantly. Thi ensures that tax timing strategies remain optimal even in dynamic environment.

Ultimately, AI transforms tax timing from an afterthought int a proactive discipline. Business owners no longer wonder wha their tax bill will be; they shape it deliberately. Timing becomes a strategic tool, not a source of anxiety. By mastering forecasting and timing with AI, businesses gain control over one of the most powerful variables in financial success — when taxes are triggered and how heavy they become.

"The Year That Didn't Crush Her"

Sophia had always dreaded December. While most people celebrated the end of the year, she braced herself for it. As the founder of a fast-growing digital design agency, her revenue surged every fourth quarter. Clients rushed to finish projects, invoices piled up, and her bank balance looked healthy — until she remembered what came next. Taxes. Every January felt like punishment for success. She paid large sums without truly understanding why, telling herself that this was simply how business worked.

One evening, exhausted after closing yet another high-value contract, Sophia logged into a new AI financial platform she had reluctantly agreed to test. She expected charts and reports. What she didn't expect was a message that read: "Your tax outcome is not inevitable." Curious, she clicked deeper.

The AI began by reconstructing her past three years. It showed her revenue spikes, expense patterns, and tax payments laid out like a story she had never read before. The system highlighted one brutal truth: Sophia's biggest tax bills were not caused by high income alone, but by poor timing. She invoiced aggressively at year-end, recognized income immediately, delayed expenses, and paid bonuses without strategy. She wasn't bad at business — she was just playing the timing game blindly.

The AI ran simulations. In one scenario, Sophia delayed certain invoices by two weeks, moving income into January. In another, she accelerated equipment purchases and software investments in December. In another, she shifted bonus payments into a retirement contribution structure. Each version produced a different tax outcome. The differences were staggering. In the optimal scenario, her tax bill dropped by nearly forty percent without changing revenue at all.

Sophia felt disbelief mixed with anger — not at the system, but at how long she had operated without visibility. She implemented the AI's recommendations cautiously at first. She adjusted invoicing practices. She aligned expenses with high-income periods. She coordinated payroll timing with cash flow forecasts. Nothing dramatic happened day to day — except that everything felt calmer.

As the months passed, the AI refined its models. When a major client requested an early invoice, the system showed Sophia the tax impact of agreeing versus delaying. When she considered hiring a new designer, it projected payroll costs across tax years. When tax laws shifted midyear, the forecasts updated automatically. Sophia stopped guessing and started deciding.

December arrived again, but this time it felt different. Sophia reviewed her dashboard and saw something she had never seen before: clarity. Her projected tax bill was known. Her cash reserves were prepared. Her deductions were already optimized. There was no panic, no scrambling, no dread.

When January came, the payment was made calmly, without shock. Sophia realized something profound in that moment. The year hadn't crushed her because she had finally learned how to control time — not by working harder, but by letting intelligence guide her decisions.

She closed her laptop, poured herself a glass of wine, and smiled. Success no longer came with fear. It came with foresight.

Chapter 6

Audit Resistance, Compliance, and Building a Business the IRS Ignores

The ultimate goal of any advanced tax strategy is not merely to reduce taxes, but to do so in a way that is invisible, defensible, and sustainable. The most dangerous misconception among business owners is that lower taxes automatically increase audit risk. In reality, audits are triggered not by low tax bills, but by inconsistency, poor documentation, mismatched reporting, and structural red flags. Artificial intelligence transforms compliance from a reactive chore into a proactive shield, ensuring that tax optimization and audit resistance grow together rather than in opposition. When AI is properly integrated into a business's financial architecture, the result is not just tax savings, but a business profile that quietly blends into statistical normalcy while operating at peak efficiency.

The IRS and other tax authorities rely heavily on pattern recognition. They compare businesses against industry averages, peer benchmarks, and historical norms to identify anomalies. AI understands these same patterns — often more precisely than human auditors — and uses them to guide business behavior into statistically defensible ranges. This does not mean underperforming or hiding income. It means structuring compensation, deductions, and entity flows in ways that align with established norms for similar businesses. AI continuously evaluates ratios such as salary-to-profit, deductions-to-revenue, and expense categories to ensure that nothing stands out as unusual. A business optimized by AI does not look aggressive; it looks ordinary, which is the safest profile of all.

Documentation is the foundation of audit resistance. Many businesses fail audits not because they claimed improper deductions, but because they cannot prove them. Receipts are missing. Contracts are vague. Intercompany payments are undocumented. AI eliminates these weaknesses by automatically generating, categorizing, and storing documentation in real time. Management fees are supported by service agreements. Licensing payments are backed by valuation models. Expense reimbursements are logged with digital evidence. Every transaction leaves a trail that can be reconstructed instantly if questioned. This transforms audits from stressful investigations into routine confirmations.

AI also enforces internal consistency across all filings. One of the most common audit triggers is mismatched data — income reported differently on tax returns, payroll filings, sales tax reports, or financial statements. AI cross-checks every report before submission, flagging discrepancies before they become problems. This level of synchronization is nearly impossible manually, especially as businesses grow across states and entities. With AI, compliance becomes automatic rather than aspirational.

Another powerful compliance advantage is proactive error correction. AI identifies potential issues early, such as excessive distributions, underreported payroll, or deductions that exceed safe thresholds. Instead of discovering these problems during an audit, businesses correct them quietly in advance. This reduces penalties, interest, and scrutiny while reinforcing long-term stability. AI does not wait for mistakes to become visible; it prevents them from forming.

Audit resistance also depends on narrative coherence. Every business tells a financial story through its numbers. If that story does not make sense — if income, expenses, and structure do not align — auditors take notice. AI ensures that the story is logical, consistent, and supported by operational reality. Compensation reflects work performed. Deductions align with business activities. Entity structures reflect functional separation. This coherence creates confidence in the eyes of regulators and reduces the likelihood of further inquiry.

The most powerful aspect of AI-driven compliance is psychological. Business owners who fear audits often avoid legitimate tax strategies out of caution, leaving enormous savings on the table. AI removes this fear by replacing uncertainty with clarity. Owners know exactly why each strategy works, how it is documented, and how it appears externally. Confidence replaces anxiety, and optimization becomes sustainable rather than stressful.

Ultimately, AI enables businesses to operate in the optimal zone where taxes are minimized, compliance is maximized, and scrutiny is unlikely. This is the quiet power of intelligent tax architecture. The goal is not to fight the system, but to understand it so completely that the business moves through it unnoticed, protected by precision, consistency, and transparency.

"The Audit That Never Came"

For years, Daniel lived with a constant, low-level fear. Every time the mail arrived, he half-expected to see an envelope marked with government insignia. As the owner of a growing construction services firm, he had heard too many horror stories — audits that dragged on for years, penalties that wiped out savings, businesses destroyed not by wrongdoing, but by chaos. Daniel wasn't dishonest. He simply felt exposed. His company made good money, claimed legitimate deductions, and operated legally, yet everything felt fragile.

Daniel's fear wasn't irrational. His business had grown faster than his systems. Expenses were tracked inconsistently. Intercompany payments were informal. Payroll decisions were made based on cash flow rather than strategy. Each year, his accountant "cleaned things up" at tax time, but Daniel sensed that the cleanup itself was a red flag. He felt like a homeowner constantly patching cracks in a foundation that was slowly shifting beneath him.

The turning point came when a colleague mentioned using AI for compliance, not just taxes. Skeptical but desperate for peace of mind, Daniel agreed to test the system. The onboarding process was meticulous. The AI examined years of financial data, entity structures, payroll records, and filings. It didn't accuse or alarm — it analyzed. Then it presented Daniel with a single summary: "Your risk is not high, but your visibility is." That sentence stayed with him.

The AI explained that Daniel's problem wasn't illegal behavior, but inconsistency. His compensation didn't align cleanly with industry benchmarks. His deductions were legitimate but poorly narrated. His intercompany payments lacked formal structure. None of these alone would trigger an audit, but together they created noise — and noise attracts attention. Over the next months, the AI quietly reorganized Daniel's financial world. Contracts were generated where handshakes had existed. Documentation flowed automatically into categorized archives. Payroll adjusted gradually into a defensible range. Intercompany transactions were priced, logged, and justified. Nothing dramatic changed in Daniel's day-to-day work, yet everything changed beneath the surface.

What surprised Daniel most was how normal his business began to look — not smaller, not weaker, but statistically ordinary. The AI showed him comparisons to peer businesses in his industry. His ratios aligned. His filings matched. His reports told a coherent story. The system wasn't making him invisible by hiding information — it was making him invisible by making sense.

Months passed. Then a year. Then another. Each tax season arrived quietly and left without drama. Daniel realized one afternoon that he no longer checked the mail with anxiety. The fear that had once hovered over every financial decision had faded, replaced by a calm certainty.

One evening, while reviewing his dashboard, Daniel noticed a metric labeled "Audit Probability." It had steadily declined over time until it rested in a zone marked "Statistically

Unlikely." He laughed softly, not because he felt invincible, but because he finally felt normal. The audit never came. Not because Daniel avoided taxes, and not because he took fewer deductions, but because his business had learned how to exist within the system intelligently. He had stopped fighting uncertainty and started designing clarity. And in doing so, he discovered that the safest business is not the one that hides — it is the one that makes perfect sense.

Chapter 7

Turning Tax Strategy Into a Permanent System

The final evolution of tax optimization is not a tactic, structure, or loophole — it is a system. Most businesses fail to achieve lasting tax efficiency because they treat strategy as a one-time event rather than a living framework. They restructure once, optimize once, or plan once, then return to autopilot until the next tax season shock. Artificial intelligence fundamentally changes this pattern by transforming tax strategy into a continuously operating system that evolves alongside the business. Instead of reacting to changes, AI anticipates them, ensuring that entity structures, compensation models, profit-shielding mechanisms, and compliance protocols remain aligned with real-world conditions at all times.

A permanent tax system begins with integration. Revenue, payroll, expenses, forecasting, compliance, and strategic planning cannot exist in isolation if tax efficiency is the goal. AI integrates these elements into a unified financial nervous system. When income rises, compensation adjusts. When expenses shift, deductions rebalance. When new jurisdictions are added, entity efficiency is recalculated. This integration eliminates the lag that traditionally causes businesses t overpay taxes simply because decisions were made without ful visibility.

One of the most powerful features of a systemized approach i feedback loops. AI constantly compares expected outcomes t actual results. If a strategy underperforms, it is corrected. If a structure becomes inefficient due to growth or legal changes, i is redesigned. This creates a self-optimizing environmen where tax strategy improves over time rather than degrading Businesses no longer rely on annual reviews; they operate witl real-time intelligence.

Systemization also removes dependency on individua advisors. While accountants and attorneys remain valuable, A becomes the connective tissue that ensures advice i implemented correctly and consistently. It tracks assumptions documents decisions, and monitors results. This prevent miscommunication, oversight, and fragmentation. The business becomes resilient not because it avoids complexity but because it manages complexity intelligently.

A permanent tax system also creates strategic freedom Business owners can pursue growth opportunities without fea of unexpected tax consequences. They can acquire companies launch new products, expand internationally, or restructure ownership knowing that AI will model the tax impact before decisions are finalized. This confidence enables bolder, smarter growth.

Perhaps most importantly, systemized tax strategy aligns financial success with peace of mind. Taxes stop being a source of stress and become a controlled variable. Business owners know what to expect, why it happens, and how to influence it. This clarity allows them to focus on innovation, leadership, and long-term vision rather than compliance anxiety.

In the end, AI does not eliminate taxes — it eliminates uncertainty. It replaces fear with foresight and chaos with control. When tax strategy becomes a permanent system, success no longer feels fragile. It becomes durable, predictable, and scalable.

"The Business That Finally Felt Finished"

For nearly a decade, Marcus believed that business was supposed to feel unfinished. There was always something unresolved — an unanswered question, a looming deadline, a future problem waiting to surface. His software consulting firm was successful by any external measure. Revenue climbed steadily. Clients were loyal. His reputation was solid. Yet beneath the surface, Marcus felt like he was constantly patching leaks. Every tax season reopened old anxieties. Every growth decision carried hidden consequences. No matter how well the business performed, it never felt complete.

Marcus had tried everything. New accountants. New bookkeeping systems. New entity structures. Each change brought temporary relief, followed by new complications. One advisor optimized his taxes but ignored cash flow. Another improved compliance but increased Marcus's tax bill. Another proposed aggressive strategies that made Marcus uneasy. The business felt like a machine assembled from mismatched parts.

The shift began when Marcus adopted an AI-driven tax and financial system not as a tool, but as infrastructure. The onboarding process forced him to confront the truth: his business wasn't broken — it was fragmented. Decisions were made in isolation. Strategies overlapped without coordination. No one, including Marcus, could see the entire picture at once.

The AI rebuilt that picture. It mapped every entity, income stream, payroll decision, expense category, and compliance obligation into a single model. Marcus watched as the system simulated future scenarios — growth, contraction, expansion, exit. For the first time, he could see not just what his business was, but what it would become.

What followed was not a dramatic overhaul, but a quiet transformation. The AI adjusted compensation gradually. It refined profit flows incrementally. It aligned documentation automatically. There was no single moment where everything changed — only a steady sense that things were finally clicking into place.

Months passed, then a year. Marcus noticed something subtle but profound: nothing surprised him anymore. Tax bills matched projections. Cash reserves behaved predictably. Growth decisions felt informed rather than risky. The business no longer demanded constant vigilance. It ran — not recklessly, but intelligently.

One evening, Marcus reviewed his dashboard and realized that there were no red alerts, no warnings, no unresolved tasks. Everything was accounted for. Optimized. Defensible. He felt something unfamiliar — completion.

Not an end, but a foundation. The business finally felt finished in the way a well-designed building feels finished — solid, adaptable, and built to last. Marcus leaned back in his chair and smiled. Success no longer felt temporary. It felt engineered.

Chapter 8

Scaling Without Penalty: How AI Protects Tax Efficiency as You Grow

Growth is often portrayed as the ultimate reward in business, yet for many companies, growth quietly becomes a punishment. Revenue increases, teams expand, markets widen — and suddenly taxes surge, compliance complexity explodes, and profit margins shrink. What once worked efficiently at a smaller scale begins to fracture under the weight of expansion. This is not because growth is flawed, but because most businesses scale operations faster than they scale financial architecture. Artificial intelligence solves this problem by ensuring that tax efficiency, entity design, and profit shielding scale *with* the business rather than collapsing beneath it. AI allows companies to grow without triggering unnecessary tax penalties, structural inefficiencies, or regulatory exposure.

One of the most dangerous myths in business is that tax strategy naturally improves as revenue increases. In reality, growth often magnifies inefficiencies. A structure that saves money at $200,000 in revenue may become disastrous at $2 million. Payroll thresholds change. Deduction limitations appear. State nexus rules activate. International reporting requirements emerge. Without AI, businesses often discover these issues only after they have already caused damage. AI anticipates these thresholds in advance. It identifies when growth will trigger new tax obligations and redesigns structures proactively so that expansion remains profitable rather than punitive.

As businesses scale, complexity increases nonlinearly. New employees, new locations, new revenue streams, and new compliance rules interact in unpredictable ways. AI excels in this environment because it thrives on complexity rather than avoiding it. It models how each growth decision affects tax exposure across all entities and jurisdictions. When a business adds a new state, AI recalculates nexus, payroll taxes, and sales tax obligations. When a new product line launches, it evaluates whether income should flow through an existing entity or a new one. This ensures that growth decisions are informed by their full financial impact rather than optimism alone.

Another critical challenge of scaling is margin compression. Many businesses grow revenue while unknowingly sacrificing profit due to rising taxes and inefficient structures. AI monitors after-tax margins continuously, highlighting when growth is eroding efficiency rather than enhancing it. It identifies whether profits are better reinvested, deferred, or restructured through different entities. This keeps growth aligned with wealth creation rather than vanity metrics. Ownership and equity changes also become more common as businesses scale. New partners, investors, or shareholders introduce additional tax complexity. AI models ownership changes before they occur, showing how equity splits, distributions, and exit scenarios will be taxed. This allows founders to negotiate from a position of clarity rather than hope. Growth becomes strategic rather than reactive.

Scaling also increases audit visibility. Larger businesses naturally attract more attention, but AI mitigates this risk by ensuring that growth remains statistically coherent. As revenue increases, deductions, payroll, and distributions scale proportionally and defensibly. This consistency reduces red flags and maintains audit resistance even at higher levels of success.

Perhaps the most powerful advantage of AI-driven scaling is optionality. Businesses can grow aggressively, conservatively, or opportunistically because AI provides real-time visibility into tax consequences. Leaders are no longer forced to choose between growth and control. They can have both.

In the end, scaling without penalty is not about avoiding taxes — it is about evolving intelligently. AI ensures that as the business grows in size, its tax strategy grows in sophistication.

Expansion becomes a source of strength rather than stress, allowing businesses to reach their full potential without sacrificing the profits they worked so hard to build.

"The Year Growth Almost Broke Them"

When Olivia and her brother Ethan launched their specialty food manufacturing company, success arrived faster than either of them expected. What began as a regional operation supplying local restaurants quickly attracted national attention. Within three years, they were shipping products across multiple states, hiring aggressively, and negotiating with major distributors. Revenue tripled in a single year. From the outside, it looked like a dream.

Inside the business, panic quietly took root.

Payroll ballooned. Sales tax notices began arriving from unfamiliar states. Their once-simple accounting system struggled to keep up. Worst of all, their tax projections suddenly made no sense. Despite record revenue, profits felt thinner. Cash reserves fluctuated unpredictably. Their accountant warned them that growth had triggered new compliance obligations — some retroactive. Olivia lay awake at night wondering how success had become so exhausting.

The breaking point came when they received a letter from a state they had never physically operated in, asserting tax nexus and demanding back filings. Olivia felt sick. Ethan was furious. They had done nothing intentionally wrong, yet they were being penalized for growing too fast without the right systems in place.

Desperate for clarity, Olivia turned to an AI-driven financial and tax platform recommended by a logistics partner. The system absorbed their data and began modeling their growth trajectory. The results were sobering. The AI showed that their original entity structure — perfectly adequate at small scale — was now actively harming them. Income was flowing inefficiently. Payroll was misaligned. Sales tax exposure was unmanaged. Growth had outpaced design.

But the AI didn't stop at diagnosis. It presented a roadmap.

The system proposed restructuring operations into regional entities to manage nexus exposure. It recommended separating manufacturing, distribution, and branding functions to optimize tax treatment. It adjusted payroll timing and compensation structures to stabilize cash flow. Most importantly, it forecasted future growth and redesigned the system to handle it gracefully.

Implementing the changes was not easy, but it was controlled.

The AI guided each step, ensuring compliance and documentation at every stage. Within months, chaos gave way to clarity. Tax notices stopped arriving unexpectedly. Cash flow stabilized. Profit margins recovered.

The true test came the following year when revenue surged again. This time, there was no panic. The AI had already anticipated the increase and adjusted structures in advance. What once felt like a crisis now felt routine.

One evening, after reviewing updated projections, Olivia realized something remarkable. Growth no longer scared her. It didn't feel like a threat waiting to expose weaknesses. It felt like momentum — something the business could absorb without breaking.

The year growth almost broke them became the year they learned how to scale intelligently. And from that point on, success no longer came with consequences — it came with control.

Chapter 9

Exit Planning, Wealth Transfer, and AI-Guided Tax Outcomes

Every business journey eventually arrives at the same question: *What happens when you step away?* Whether the goal is to sell, merge, pass the business to family, or simply reduce involvement while retaining income, exit planning is the moment when tax strategy reveals its true power. A poorly planned exit can erase decades of hard work in a single transaction, while a well-designed one can multiply wealth, preserve legacy, and protect future generations. Artificial intelligence transforms exit planning from a distant afterthought into an integrated, forward-looking discipline that shapes decisions years before an exit ever occurs. Instead of reacting to tax consequences at the moment of sale or transfer, AI allows business owners to design their desired outcome long in advance.

Traditional exit planning is often reactive. Business owners approach advisors when a buyer appears or when retirement is near, only to discover that their entity structure, compensation history, and asset placement are misaligned with optimal tax treatment. At that point, options are limited. AI changes this by continuously modeling exit scenarios as the business operates. It evaluates how current decisions affect futur outcomes, showing whether income should be reinvested distributed, or shielded in anticipation of a sale or transfer This long-range visibility allows business owners to shape their financial destiny instead of surrendering it to timing and circumstance.

One of the most significant tax variables in an exit is how value is characterized. Is the value in operating income, intellectual property, goodwill, or physical assets? Each is taxed differently. AI dissects the business into its value components and identifies where wealth is accumulating. It then recommends structural adjustments that shift value into more tax-efficient categories over time. For example, separating intellectual property into its own entity years before a sale can dramatically change how proceeds are taxed. Without AI these strategies are often overlooked until it is too late.

AI also models buyer behavior. Different buyers value different aspects of a business. Strategic buyers may prioritize intellectual property and market position, while financial buyers focus on cash flow and margins. AI simulates how various buyer types would structure a deal and how each structure affects taxes. This allows business owners to position their companies to attract favorable offers while minimizing tax exposure. Exit planning becomes proactive marke positioning rather than passive hope. Wealth transfer introduces another layer of complexity. Passing a business to heirs or partners involves gift taxes, estate taxes, valuation rules, and succession planning. AI evaluates these factors holistically, showing how ownership can be transferred gradually, strategically, and tax-efficiently. It models lifetime gifting strategies, trusts, and entity restructuring to preserve wealth while maintaining control during the owner's lifetime. This transforms succession from a legal headache into a carefully orchestrated process.

Timing is again critical. The year of exit, the method of payment, and the structure of proceeds all influence tax outcomes. AI forecasts future tax environments, projecting how rates, exemptions, and regulations may evolve. While no forecast is perfect, AI provides a probabilistic framework that helps business owners choose timing windows with confidence rather than speculation. This reduces regret and maximizes retained wealth.

Perhaps the most overlooked aspect of exit planning is emotional readiness. Many business owners delay planning because confronting an exit feels like admitting the end of an identity. AI reframes exit planning as continuity rather than conclusion. It shows how strategic decisions today create options tomorrow. Whether the owner exits fully, partially, or not at all, the business becomes a vehicle for long-term security rather than a single event.

Ultimately, AI-guided exit planning ensures that the final chapter of a business story is written intentionally. Wealth is preserved. Taxes are minimized. Legacy is protected. And the transition becomes a culmination of intelligent design rather than a scramble for damage control.

"The Deal That Changed Everything"

For most of her career, Linda told herself she would think about selling her company "someday." She built a respected environmental consulting firm from scratch, pouring twenty-five years into its growth. The company employed dozens of specialists, worked with major municipalities, and generated steady profits. Yet Linda avoided conversations about exit planning. The business was not just her livelihood — it was her identity.

The conversation she could no longer avoid arrived in the form of an email. A national firm expressed interest in acquiring her company. The offer was flattering, but it filled Linda with unease. She had no idea what the deal would mean for her financially. Would she lose half of it to taxes? Would her employees be safe? Would she regret selling too early — or too late?

Linda's accountant urged caution. Her attorney warned about complexity. Each advisor focused on a narrow slice of the problem. Feeling overwhelmed, Linda agreed to use an AI-driven exit planning platform recommended by a trusted peer. She expected projections. What she received was perspective.

The AI began by reconstructing Linda's business history. It analyzed how value had accumulated over time and where it currently lived within the company. The results surprised her. Much of the company's value was tied to proprietary methodologies and long-standing contracts — intellectual assets she had never formally separated. The AI showed that if she sold the business as-is, those assets would be taxed unfavorably.

Then the system showed an alternative future.

By restructuring ownership of intellectual property over the next eighteen months, adjusting compensation patterns, and repositioning goodwill, Linda could significantly reduce the tax impact of a sale. The AI simulated multiple exit scenarios: an immediate sale, a partial sale, a staged earn-out, and a family succession. Each path carried different emotional and financial outcomes.

Linda realized something she had never considered: she didn't have to decide everything at once. Exit planning was not a single decision — it was a sequence. Over the next year, Linda implemented the AI's recommendations. The changes were subtle but powerful. Value shifted. Documentation improved. Options expanded. When the acquiring firm returned with a revised offer, Linda was ready. She understood the structure, the tax implications, and the long-term impact.

The deal closed on terms that felt fair — not just financially, but personally. Linda retained a consulting role, ensured continuity for her employees, and preserved far more wealth than she had imagined possible. Taxes were no longer an unpleasant surprise; they were a managed outcome.

Months later, sitting in her garden with time she had never allowed herself before, Linda reflected on the experience. The business had not ended her story — it had enabled the next chapter. And because she had planned intelligently, that chapter began with freedom rather than regret.

The deal that once terrified her became the decision that changed everything — not because it was perfect, but because it was intentional.

Chapter 10

The Future-Proof Business: Designing Tax Strategy That Survives Change

The final test of any tax strategy is not how well it performs today, but how well it survives tomorrow. Tax laws change. Economies shift. Technologies disrupt entire industries. Businesses that rely on static strategies eventually find themselves outdated, exposed, and overtaxed. The purpose of artificial intelligence in tax optimization is not merely to reduce taxes in the present moment, but to create structures that adapt automatically as conditions evolve. A future-proof business is one whose tax architecture is flexible, responsive, and resilient — capable of absorbing change without collapsing into inefficiency or risk.

Traditional tax planning assumes stability. Advisors build strategies around current laws, current income, and current business models. When any of those variables change, the strategy breaks. AI eliminates this fragility by continuously monitoring internal performance and external conditions. It tracks regulatory changes, court rulings, industry benchmarks, and economic indicators, recalibrating recommendations in real time. This transforms tax strategy from a brittle framework into a dynamic system that evolves alongside th business.

One of the greatest threats to long-term tax efficiency is scal mismatch. As businesses grow, their tax needs change faste than their structures. What once saved money begins to creat penalties. What once protected assets becomes restrictive. A identifies these inflection points early. It detects when a entity has outlived its usefulness, when compensatio strategies need recalibration, or when profit-shieldin mechanisms require redesign. Instead of reacting to problem after they surface, AI prevents them by evolving the systen continuously.

Technological disruption also reshapes tax realities Automation, remote work, digital products, and globa commerce introduce new tax challenges and opportunities. A understands these shifts natively. It models how digita revenue is taxed differently from physical goods, how remot teams affect nexus and payroll obligations, and how emergin regulations may impact future profits. This foresight allow businesses to adopt new technologies without fear o unintended tax consequences.

Another pillar of future-proofing is optionality. Businesse should never be locked into a single outcome. AI-driven ta systems preserve flexibility by maintaining clean separation between entities, assets, and income streams. This allows businesses to pivot, divest, acquire, or exit without triggering catastrophic tax events. Optionality is not indecision — it is strategic freedom.

Future-proofing also extends beyond the business itself to the owner's personal wealth. AI aligns business tax strategy with personal financial planning, retirement goals, and legacy objectives. This ensures that success inside the company translates into long-term security outside it. The business becomes a tool for wealth creation rather than a liability that demands constant attention.

Perhaps the most important benefit of AI-driven future-proofing is psychological. Business owners who fear change often resist growth or innovation. AI removes this fear by providing visibility and control. Owners know that no matter how the landscape shifts, their systems will adapt. Confidence replaces hesitation. Vision replaces anxiety.

In the end, the future-proof business is not one that predicts the future perfectly, but one that is designed to respond intelligently. Artificial intelligence makes this possible. It ensures that tax strategy is not a constraint on growth, but a foundation that supports it indefinitely. The business becomes more than profitable — it becomes durable.

"The Last Time He Worried About Taxes"

Ethan had spent most of his adult life worrying. Not the kind of worry that paralyzes, but the kind that hums constantly in the background. As the founder of a multi-entity technology services company, he worried about cash flow, employees, clients, and competition. But above all, he worried about taxes. Every year brought a new surprise. New rules. New penalties. New confusion. No matter how successful the business became, uncertainty followed him like a shadow.

Ethan told himself this was normal. Business was supposed to be stressful. Success came with complexity. Still, he couldn't shake the feeling that he was always one step behind — reacting instead of leading. When a trusted advisor suggested implementing an AI-driven tax and financial system, Ethan hesitated. He had already invested in software, consultants, and restructures that promised clarity but delivered fragmentation. This time felt different, though. The promise wasn't optimization — it was continuity.

The AI didn't start by offering solutions. It started by asking questions about the future. Where did Ethan want the business to be in five years? Ten? Did he plan to sell, scale, or step back? Did he want income now or later? Did he value simplicity or optionality? No advisor had ever asked him these questions in this way. The system wasn't trying to fix the past — it was designing the future.

As the AI mapped Ethan's business, it revealed a sobering truth. His company wasn't inefficient — it was frozen in time. Structures built years earlier were still in place, long after they stopped making sense. Compensation strategies hadn't evolved with revenue. Profit-shielding mechanisms were outdated. Nothing was wrong yet — but everything was vulnerable.

Over the following months, the AI quietly rebuilt the foundation. Entities were simplified where complexity added no value and expanded where flexibility mattered. Income streams were reorganized. Documentation was standardized. Forecasts updated continuously. There was no dramatic overhaul, no sleepless nights. Just steady alignment.

Then change came — as it always does.

A major regulatory shift affected one of Ethan's core revenue streams. Competitors panicked. Advisors scrambled. Ethan watched his dashboard update calmly. The AI had already modeled this scenario. Adjustments were recommended automatically. Income was rerouted. Exposure was reduced. What could have been a crisis became a footnote.

More changes followed. A new market opportunity emerged overseas. AI modeled the tax implications instantly. Ethan expanded with confidence. A potential acquisition appeared. The system evaluated the structure before negotiations even began. Decisions felt informed, not rushed.

One evening, years after implementing the system, Ethan realized something unsettling — and liberating. He couldn't remember the last time he worried about taxes. Not because he ignored them, but because they no longer surprised him. They behaved predictably. Intelligently. Quietly.

Sitting alone in his office after everyone had gone home, Ethan reflected on how much energy he had wasted fearing the unknown. The business had always been strong. What it lacked was adaptability. AI hadn't eliminated taxes. It had eliminated fragility.

Ethan shut down his computer and smiled. Tomorrow would bring new challenges — it always would. But for the first time, he knew that whatever came next, his business was ready.

And that was the last time he worried about taxes.

Final Thoughts

From Tax Survival to Strategic Control

The journey through this book has not been about discoverin tricks, shortcuts, or loopholes. It has been about something fa more powerful: understanding that taxes are not a unavoidable consequence of success, but a system that reward foresight, structure, and intelligence. For most busines owners, taxes have always felt like gravity — constant, heavy and impossible to escape. Artificial intelligence changes tha relationship entirely. It does not remove gravity, but it allow you to build wings. When tax strategy becomes intelligent adaptive, and systemic, success no longer carries fear with it.

Throughout this book, you have seen how AI transforms ta planning from a reactive annual event into a living financia architecture. You have learned that entity selection is not a one-time decision, but an evolving identity that must grov with the business. You have seen how compensation desig determines whether income is punished or rewarded. Yo have explored profit shielding, timing, forecasting compliance, scaling, exit planning, and future-proofing — no as isolated tactics, but as interlocking components of a unifie system. When these elements operate together, taxes sto draining momentum and start reinforcing it.

One of the most important realizations is that complexity itself is not the enemy. Poorly managed complexity is. Modern businesses are inherently complex. They operate across platforms, jurisdictions, and revenue models that did not exist a generation ago. Artificial intelligence thrives in this complexity. It sees patterns where humans see noise. It identifies inefficiencies long before they become expensive. It adapts continuously without emotional bias. This is why AI is not just a tool in tax optimization — it is the missing infrastructure.

Another critical shift this book invites you to make is psychological. Fear is the silent tax that most entrepreneurs pay. Fear of audits. Fear of penalties. Fear of growth. Fear of making the wrong move. AI replaces fear with visibility. When you can see the consequences of decisions before you make them, uncertainty dissolves. Confidence grows. Business owners stop shrinking their ambitions to fit outdated systems and start building systems that support their ambitions instead.

This book has also emphasized that ethical optimization is not only possible — it is preferable. The strongest tax strategies are not aggressive or hidden. They are logical, documented, defensible, and aligned with economic reality. AI ensures that strategies remain inside safe statistical norms while still capturing every legal advantage available. This balance is what allows optimization to scale without risk and survive regulatory scrutiny over time.

Perhaps the most enduring lesson is that tax strategy should never be separated from long-term vision. Businesses that optimize only for this year sacrifice flexibility tomorrow. Businesses that design with the future in mind gain optionality — the freedom to grow, pivot, sell, or step back without financial damage. AI enables this by continuously modeling future outcomes and aligning present decisions with them. The result is not just lower taxes, but better choices.

As you move forward, remember that implementation is not about perfection. It is about progression. The power of an AI-driven system lies in its ability to improve continuously. Each adjustment compounds. Each optimization strengthens the whole. Over time, what begins as tax efficiency becomes financial resilience, strategic clarity, and personal peace of mind.

This book closes one volume of the series, but it opens a new way of thinking. When taxes are no longer something you endure, but something you design, business stops feeling fragile. Success stops feeling temporary. And wealth stops leaking away unseen.

You are no longer reacting to the system. You are operating within it — intelligently.

www.ingramcontent.com/pod-product-compliance
Ingram Content Group UK Ltd.
Pitfield, Milton Keynes, MK11 3LW, UK
UKHW020155290926
15471UKWH00005B/894